DELIVERING TRAINING COURSES

A PRACTICAL GUIDE FOR THOSE NEW TO BUSINESS TRAINING

Edited by Helen Jamieson

© **Copyright Jaluch Limited 2013**

Published by:
Jaluch Limited, Jaluch House, Deweys Lane, Ringwood, Hants BH24 1AJ, UK.

Delivering Training Courses: A practical guide for those new to business training. First edition.

Visit us at: http://www.jaluch.co.uk

T: +44(0)1425 479888   **E**: help@jaluch.co.uk

Authors: Helen Jamieson and Lesley Wheeler
Design and layout: Elizabeth McDonald

All rights reserved. No part of this work may be reproduced, stored in a retrieval system, or transmitted in any form or by any means, electronic, mechanical photocopying, recording, or otherwise, without prior permission of the copyright owner.

CONTENTS

Introduction

9 **Training in the workplace**
- Teacher or trainer?
- Trainer or facilitator?
- Hitting the mark
- Learning difficulties
- Disabilities
- Language barriers
- Numeracy and literacy

16 **Preparing to train**
- Before you start
- One week before
- Personal preparation
- Materials
- Timing
- Checklist for opening a course

28 **Presentation skills**
- Masking your nerves
- Using your voice
- Using silence
- Body language
- Use of flipcharts
- Use of equipment
- Presentation of exercises

43 **Managing your delegates**
- Understanding the different types of delegate
- Involving delegates
- Energising a group
- Dealing with conflict
- Questions - and answers!

Managing a learning environment
Ways to split a group
Other things to consider
Running exercises and activities
Scenarios and roleplays

 Icebreakers and energisers
Introduction
Tower of trouble
Unconcious bias - it's not a game!
Down the mountain
Wallpaper
Candidate search

 And finally...

INTRODUCTION

This Trainers' Guide is designed for those who are new to delivering training. It provides handy tips and information to help you prepare for and deliver, or facilitate training. We all have doubts about our ability at times and there is nothing more nerve-racking than putting yourself in front of a group of people who have high expectations. But the only way to build your confidence is self-belief, preparation and practice!

Consider this Guide as part of your 'preparation' before you step in front of your delegates! We hope you find it useful. However, should there be any sections missing that you would have found helpful, then please email us (help@jaluch.co.uk) to let us know and we can add them in. Equally, if you have feedback on any parts of the guide, we look forward to hearing it. We believe that in everything we do continual improvement is important.

A short note about trends in training

Over the past 5-10 years, we have seen quite a change in how training is delivered within organisations.

10 years ago, it would not have been uncommon for someone to attend a three or five day training course to learn how to better hold staff appraisals, or do competency based interviewing.

You might even have attended a two week residential training course to develop management skills. But in recent years there have been a number of notable trends.

- Surprising as it may seem, **continuous professional development** (CPD) is a relatively new term and concept. We now take the view that our development is an ongoing process throughout our careers.
- There has been a move away from face-to-face training sessions, to an approach that is commonly termed **'blended learning'**. We talk more about this later.
- Some face-to-face training has been totally replaced with **e-learning** activities.

- There has been a move towards **shorter learning sessions** sometimes called 'toolbox talks', or 'lunchtime learners' which shows it is now quite unusual for staff to be taken away from their jobs for more than half a day at a time.
- Far more courses are being **formally accredited** - with accreditation being sought from bodies such as the ILM. Credits from attending courses can often be put towards more formal qualifications if the delegate wishes to do so.
- In 2013 alone, it was estimated that **44% more organisations were bringing their training in house**, using external trainers less and, as a result, having to develop in house training skill.
- There has also been a significant move towards **individuals taking responsibility** for their own learning, rather than relying on their organisations to develop their skills and knowledge.

As a direct result of these changes, there are now numerous individuals who are being asked to deliver training alongside carrying out their normal day to day roles. Although many organisations do still have an internal training function, more and more training delivery is being passed to managers and experts within organisations to deliver.

But whether you work full time in training or are just required to deliver the occasional training course, this guide has been designed for you!

An opportunity to deliver training... so what might be in it for you?

- Opportunity to develop a new skill
- Platform to extend your management/business knowledge
- Personal positioning to gain recognition from colleagues and managers
- Personal development and confidence building
- Increased variety in your work

- Opportunity to broaden your career and enhance your CV
- Important step in building a business/personal network

And what are the benefits for employers in developing in-house training skills?

- Maximises use of internal time resources
- Develops/enhances skill set of existing staff
- Provides trainers/facilitators who easily understand internal commercial issues and drivers
- Reduces spend with external suppliers (training organisations)
- For those seeking greater variety in their work, it creates the ability to successfully manage different duties
- Provides job opportunities for ambitious staff in organisations with flat structures
- Offers greater flexibility to deliver multiple one or two hour sessions, rather than be restricted to whole day training sessions provided by external suppliers

TEACHER OR TRAINER?

Being a trainer in the workplace is very different from being a teacher in a school environment.

Key things to remember:

1. Most employees are adults and want to be treated like adults in the training environment. Many adults particularly don't like being talked 'at'.

2. School teachers know that children have to turn up tomorrow even if they didn't like your lesson today. However, in the workplace, your delegates won't turn up next time if they don't buy in to what (or how) you deliver this time. No pressure then!

3. Very few workplaces currently favour a chalk and talk approach, which is old style 'teaching'. Variety, participation and experiential learning (learning by doing) are far more the norm. Eye glazing PowerPoints are often just for the lazy.

4. Employees like and need to understand how what they are learning relates to the jobs they do, therefore you need to continually make it as relevant as possible.

5. Trainers are often simply facilitators to a discussion, rather than being the ultimate authority on a subject. They raise topics, pass on knowledge and then provide the opportunity to discuss, debate and learn.

6. Teachers are often constrained in what they can do by the parameters of the curriculum. Trainers usually have much more flexibility to morph and adapt their training as they go in order to ensure it reflects as closely as possible the needs of the delegates (and organisation).

> "Tell me and I forget. Teach me and I remember.
> Involve me and I learn."

TRAINER OR FACILITATOR?

Many ask where the differences lie between training and facilitating.

Training can be defined in many ways. Often though, we think of it as the delivery of organised activities that are designed to impart information or instructions. It is not uncommon that a trainer will lead delegates towards a certain understanding or predetermined answers.

In contrast, a facilitator is someone who tends to support delegates learning without taking a particular position. The outcome is therefore not pre-determined.

During a training course there may be times when the trainer moves between these two roles.

The skills of a good facilitator include:

- Patience
- Great listening skills
- Ability to keep group to order and to time
- Ability to summarise the discussion and regularly check back on understanding
- Ability to involve all delegates and draw out those who contribute less
- Ability to resist the temptation to take control

HITTING THE MARK

In order to satisfy the differing needs and preferred learning styles of the employees you are training and ensure you hit the mark first time, you might consider incorporating:

Materials and activities that require delegates to use different senses:

- **Vision** – pictures, images, graphs, charts, drawings, video
- **Hearing** – words, sounds, music, conversation
- **Taste** – foods and drinks can be incorporated into exercises
- **Smell** – foods, drinks, flora and fauna

Using **recap and recall** throughout the learning process to accommodate both those who like to reflect and also those who struggle to concentrate or listen.

Mixing up **sedentary** activities with those that require delegates to be on their feet.

Alternative exercises/options to draw on if necessary to accommodate those who arrive and say that they have mobility issues, hearing, concentration or sight issues etc.

Providing links to **further reading** for those who like to see the research/in-depth analysis.

Providing **pre-course work** and sending agendas out in advance, for those who like to reflect and mentally prepare themselves before arriving for training.

Keeping the **written materials easy to follow.** As a rule of thumb, use short words, easy phrases, short sentences and have only two or three sentences in a paragraph. Allow plenty of space on their written materials for delegates to write their own notes.

Changing the **pace** at different times in the training to accommodate both those who like to spend more time reflecting and also those who like to keep moving on very quickly.

Diagrams and pictures to support those who either struggle to read (or write) or who don't have English as a first language.

Technology to keep things current and modern. Options are e-learning modules, use of YouTube or audio clips, using phone apps, online quizzes, computer simulation exercises etc.

Experiential learning activities to reinforce learning and provide opportunities to demonstrate the application of learning.

Kinaesthetic learners learn most effectively through imitation and practice. They do not learn so effectively with traditional training medium such as listening (to the trainer), watching (PowerPoints etc) and reading (delegate packs). Kinaesthetic learners make up around 5% of the population.

THINGS TO REMEMBER

- Just because you like to learn in one way does not mean that your delegates will all like to learn in the same way.

- When putting together training, or delivering training, you cannot afford to assume your way is best and that delegates will just have to fit in.

LEARNING DIFFICULTIES

The information in this section relates to the United Kingdom. If you are outside the UK, hopefully you will already have some understanding of the learning difficulties you are likely to face amongst your delegates. Key areas to consider are:

- National statistics on learning difficulties
- National information on disabilities
- Numbers of delegates who do not have your language as their first language
- Numeracy and literacy rates

A little note about learning difficulties in the UK

Figures vary, but it is thought that about 1 in 10 children in the UK has a learning difficulty (e.g. dyslexia, autism, dyspraxia, ADHD). This means that as inevitably children become adults (!) in many of your training courses you will have delegates who might find parts of the training difficult.

How are you going to accommodate them?

An overview:

Dyslexia – 4-8% of the UK population - might affect reading and writing. On the flip side they often have very good verbal skills, great visual reasoning skills, think laterally around issues and are good at understanding the big picture.

ADD or ADHD (Attention Deficit Hyperactivity Disorder) – 1.7% of the UK population - concentration issues, restless, impulsivity, personal organisation issues. On the flip side, they are often highly intelligent, think laterally, bring energy and ideas in.

Autism – 1% of the UK population - over/under sensitivity to sounds, touch, smells, light, colour. Struggle to understand feelings, assess how others are thinking. Delegates might struggle in group exercises or to participate fully in a training session. On the flip side they can be extremely intelligent, can often have intense focus on one subject others would not.

Dyspraxia — 10% of the UK population (2% severely affected) - can affect hand/eye co-ordination and balance, can affect personal organisation skills, can be distracted easily, struggle with complex instructions, have difficulty prioritising. On the flip side they can be very creative, strategic problem solvers, original thinkers.

DISABILITIES

A little note about disabilities

Before any training, it is helpful to ask delegates if they have any special requirements to make their training session successful. When you're about to start the course, encountering a disability you were not aware of can be problematic, particularly if you are training on your own.

Disabilities you are most likely to encounter include:

- Hearing difficulties
- Poor eye sight or blindness
- Mobility issues or, conversely, inability to sit down or sit still for long periods

If you're unsure of how to help, a good starting point is to ask the delegate what adjustments or support would be of value to them.

LANGUAGE BARRIERS

A little note about language barriers

It is estimated that about 8% of the population of the UK does not have English as its first language. This can impact how you deliver your learning and the activities your delegates are asked to undertake. Even when someone can speak English well, that does not mean they feel confident to write to a high standard and it does not mean they can participate in a group activity where there is the added complexity of lots of people speaking at once.

We experienced a series of training courses delivered in a London based hotel, which took into consideration the fact that 56 languages were spoken by staff. This is an extreme example, but it is not unusual to have one or more delegates who might struggle with a whole day or session of English.

A little note about numeracy and literacy

In 2011, it was estimated that 24% of adults in the UK would struggle to count to 1000. Also, 15% of adults have the reading and writing age of a child aged 11 or younger. This means they would struggle to write a short email to a colleague using the correct spelling and punctuation.

As a trainer you need to be aware of how common literacy and numeracy issues are and where necessary, adapt your training to ensure it does not embarrass or alienate those who struggle in this area.

As with so many things in business, it is good preparation that can determine your success. To get you thinking about this for a few minutes, here are a few of our tales and experiences:

TRUST

We once delivered a bullying and harassment course within an organisation. We had been told that there had been a few complaints about bullying in recent months and the organisation just felt it was a sensible time to roll out some training for managers, so everyone understood what the issues were and how to manage them properly. It all sounded very sensible. In our very first session, it quickly became apparent that the whole group was in a state of barely controlled aggression, one of the managers attending had bullied one of his employees into suicide just weeks earlier. The other managers felt that this training was a cop out on the part of the company, who didn't want to formally discipline this one manager.

While this may be an extreme example, it proves you can damage your whole training opportunity if you don't understand the full picture before you walk through the door. In this case, what we learnt was not to take on face value why a course was being organised - trust a little less, question a little more!

CLUTTER

As a trainer, you might assume when you have checked availability and booked a training space, all you need to do is turn up and deliver some great training. On one memorable occasion, we did just that. But on arrival, we found that someone had written all over the white board in a pen that could not be easily wiped off and that the whole room was so cluttered, delegates would have to climb over boxes to take their seats!

Have you any idea what it is like to spend a whole day in a room where you can barely move and there is so much clutter? There is no space to even think. Naturally, the delegates end of day feedback forms blamed the trainer's failure to book an adequate room. They saw this as the trainer's responsibility which means that **you** have to check out any facilities that have been arranged for you, **before** it is too late to change!

PREPARING TO TRAIN

THE PEOPLE

We cannot count the number of times a training course has been derailed or nearly derailed by one difficult, awkward and disruptive delegate. Sometimes you cannot plan for these individuals, but sometimes you can. It just takes the discipline to find out who is due to attend your training and to ask a little about each of them.

On one memorable occasion, an IT director attended a training course and from the very first minute it became clear that she felt this course was a waste of her precious time and that all trainers were, in her opinion, a waste of space. She went on to argue her way through the entire day, derailing each exercise and side tracking every discussion.

We have a lot of very senior people attend training but it is particularly hard to deal with their petulant behaviour when they are the most senior person in the room.

In the debrief with HR the next day, the HR manager said that she thought this particular director was going to be difficult but had decided not to raise it and thought she would just see how it all panned out! As a trainer, whenever you get the opportunity, ask about your delegates **before** your training begins.

MOBILE PHONES/DEVICES

It might seem like the last thing that should be on your mind, but managing people and their mobile devices is an essential skill and something you should consider in your preparation. A short while ago we heard about a trainer who lost all credibility within the first five minutes of the one day training course they were delivering by requiring delegates to put away their phones and mobile devices.

This dictatorial approach to mobile devices had two consequences:

1. No one had brought paper and pen to the training room so ten minutes was wasted on sourcing writing equipment for everyone.

2. Everyone in the organisation had been equipped with iPads for note taking, so requiring them to be put away seemed archaic and out of touch with modern working practices which seriously aggrieved the delegates.

BEFORE YOU START

You need:
- A budget (even if just for refreshments)
- An understanding of the course objectives
- A date/dates
- A location and room (possibly break out space as well)
- Delegates

This involves you:
- Understanding the business case for this training
- Creating or agreeing an agenda
- Creating or using pre-prepared training
- Liaising with managers around employee availability
- Booking facilities
- Writing and sending joining instructions outlining the training
- Preparing yourself

ONE WEEK BEFORE

A few ideas for you...

The room:
- Spend some time in the room where you will be training
- Consider the space each delegate has
- Consider the best place to stand (don't go on tradition)

The equipment:
- Play and get comfortable with the equipment you will be using
- Write on the flipchart and then stand back and look at it
- Buy any peripherals you need (prizes, bits for exercises, refreshments etc.)

The training content:
- Read through the course content
- Highlight the key points in your trainer notes – personalise your notes
- Run through the timings – are they realistic?
- Adapt materials to suit your style if necessary

Printing materials:
- Print materials or copy handouts

PERSONAL PREPARATION

In an ideal world...

- Watch your diet the week before you train
- Keep healthy and active
- Drink lots of water
- Try on your outfit – with accessories, e.g. tie/necklace/scarf
- Consider your usual 'look'

When you still have some time to prepare – just not as long as you would have liked

- Find some comfortable, polished shoes (or shoes acceptable for your workplace) you might find it has been a long time since you spent the whole day on your feet
- Rehearse
- Practice talking out loud and adjusting your volume/voice projection
- Practice asking questions – Why? Can you explain your thinking around that a bit more?
- Ask others about your presentation
- If your trainers notes or handouts do not have page numbers on them, now is the time to add in numbers - just in case you swipe the whole pile off your desk and have to quickly reorganise

When you are now panicking as you have run out of time to prepare...

- Keeping your energy up is a must, so have something to eat and drink
- Double check in the mirror that 'you'll do' and that you have nothing stuck between your teeth!
- Smooth down your hair, grin at yourself in the mirror
- Grab your training stuff and run!

MATERIALS

All too often trainers remember the 'big' stuff but forget the 'peripherals'.

The big stuff
- Trainer notes
- Delegate pack or handouts
- Presentation equipment – projector, laptop, screen
- PowerPoint or other presentation material

The peripherals that make your training great
(In fact they don't make your training look great, but if you forget them, they can make your training look unprofessional and unprepared).

- Name cards/badges
- Flipcharts and additional pens
- Blue Tac, Sellotape, scissors
- Extra paper and pens
- Prizes/awards
- Equipment for exercises
- Delegate list
- Additional reading material or reference material for delegates
- Refreshment and meal times detail

TIMING

This might seem trivial, but timing details are critical for every training course.

Have you ever sat in a conference that was supposed to break for lunch at 1.00pm but at 1.30pm the speaker is still ploughing through, even though no one in the audience is really concentrating any more? Don't EVER let that happen to you. Delegates can be very unforgiving if you mess up with timing – especially if they are waiting for a break to be able to eat!

Communicating timings...

- Aim to be the first to arrive and the last to leave at every training session
- Be clear in the first 10 minutes of the training about start and finish times
- Indicate where breaks will occur
- Bring with you a clock or timer that can be on your desk as a constant reminder of the time, and try to avoid looking at your watch as it distracts delegates

Keeping to time...

- Don't wait for stragglers, start on time and don't stop as they arrive
- Congratulate delegates when they keep to time
- Keep an eye on your schedule
- Be clear in your mind how long you will spend on each section
- Always overestimate the time – no one minds finishing early
- Write times into your notes
- Be firm about time allocated for activities and breaks

When it's not quite going to plan...
- Be honest when you are running late – don't apologise
- Be prepared to adapt the schedule if you overrun
- Always explain to delegates if you change the schedule
- Its fine to negotiate break lengths – but stay in charge
- Don't be afraid to politely cut individuals off if they are too talkative

Common mistakes with timing...

1. As you go, don't hesitate to judge time spent on activities against value to the delegates. Sticking to the plan is less important than delivering what delegates need.

2. Allow time for delegates to think if you have asked a question. It's so easy to leap right in and give the answer yourself, or always work to the speed of the faster thinker in the room.

3. You can't assume when you set a time to return from a break that everyone's watch is showing the same time, or indeed, that everyone has a watch.

4. If your usual delegate numbers are 12 but then one day you only have six, you need to ensure you have more material/exercises with you. Even reducing numbers by one or two can have a big impact. Equally, if you have 20 delegates next day, you need to be aware that you will get through far less than is in the training pack.

5. In a similar vein, experience has shown us that if you use the same material with different departments, sometimes this can really mess up your timings. For example those in accounts or R&D (depending on the personalities involved) are less likely to spend time debating, discussing and arguing points and will have to be dragged kicking and screaming into any role plays. In contrast, those in sales and marketing teams may well have to be broken apart when doing role play and they often love taking a very participative and vocal approach to training!

NO ONE LIKES A TRAINER WHO FINISHES LATE!

CHECKLIST FOR OPENING A COURSE

- Be prepared
- Be relaxed
- Believe in what you are doing
- Use your voice, facial expression and gestures to portray enthusiasm
- Circulate amongst delegates before the course, avoid getting 'trapped'
- Avoid any training related topic until you are ready to start (the weather, their journey, when they arrived, are all safe subjects)
- Move everyone to the training area when you are ready to start
- If using one - have the flipchart pre-prepared with title, content, timings and your name
- When everyone is ready begin by saying your name and the course title
- Welcome everyone and thank them for being there
- Say briefly what the course will cover
- Cover domestic arrangements including:

    - Timings
    - Break and lunch arrangements
    - Location of rest rooms/toilets
    - Smoking breaks
    - Switching mobile phones/devices onto silent
    - If delegates need to take calls, they should leave the room to do so
    - Fire evacuation - nearest exit/assembly point
    - Any alarm tests
    - Confidentiality and ground rules

- Don't read from notes, but don't lose the thread
- Don't spend too long on detail
- Commence round the table introductions (this might be your first icebreaker exercise)
- Don't forget to involve yourself in introductions
- Ask if anyone needs to leave early or leave the session part way through for anything
- Remember faces and names:

    ○ We often recommend that before starting you draw the outline of the desks/chairs in the room and write down each person's name against where they are sitting when you first make the introductions

    ○ Keep this diagram in front of you during the session so you can address delegates by their name...

```
Peter         Cedric
Jane          Kyle
Ali           Jessica
Ruhksana      Sam
Denise        Martin
        Me!
```

PREPARING TO TRAIN

PRESENTATION SKILLS

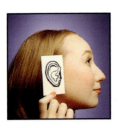  

TONE	VERBAL	BODY LANGUAGE
How we sound	The words we use	How others see us
38%	7%	55%

Words are only a fraction of the whole message we convey when we communicate. It is the sum of what we say and how we say it that delivers our message. It also dictates how others respond to us.

What are your personal strengths and weaknesses in presenting?

What my strengths are as a trainer

1.
2.
3.

What can let me down in my presentation that I would like to develop

1.
2.
3.

The following pages look at these areas:
- Masking your nerves
- Using your voice
- Using silence
- Body language
- Use of flipcharts
- Use of equipment
- Presentation of exercises

> "If you can't explain it simply, you don't understand it well enough." Albert Einstein

MASKING YOUR NERVES

It is not unusual for a trainer to feel nervous. In fact, many say that nerves can keep you on top of your game and actually help you to deliver a great course.

It is not great suffering from nerves though and it's crucial you don't let them damage your confidence or more importantly, let delegates see your nerves because as a result, they will lose confidence in you.

As a trainer, nerves might result in:

- Stomach upsets
- Shaking hands or wobbling voice
- Inability to eat beforehand
- Clumsiness
- Talking too fast
- Not listening or losing your train of thought

It's really important that you find a way to mask or control your nerves. Here are a few ideas, but ultimately you will need to find what works for you:

- Thorough preparation can help calm nerves
- Wearing loose fitting clothes can help you feel comfortable and wearing layers, so you can take one off if needed
- Deep controlled breathing before you enter the training room is often a great idea
- Giving yourself plenty of time to arrive, set up and check you have what you need
- Taking an extra five minutes in the rest room to check your appearance, calm your breathing etc. can be great

- Not worrying about food, but keeping water on your desk and a small energy bar for when you need it.
- Putting your notes on the desk to avoid any hand shakes being magnified through you holding papers that are visible to delegates.
- Prop yourself on a desk for a few minutes to avoid wobbly legs.
- Start with an icebreaker, it will put the attention on the delegates and away from you. You could do this before you go through all the introductions/housekeeping information.
- Practising a calm face in the mirror. Some even have a ritual of passing their hand across their face when they want to put their 'professional face' on.

USING YOUR VOICE

Projection - Speak slightly louder than you normally would, talk to the back of the room (this may depend on the size of the room and number of delegates).

Articulation - State each word clearly, don't shorten words, avoid personal 'tics' – ok, alright, actually, you know.

Modulation - Vary tone and pitch of voice. Be dramatic or sensitive, excited or serious depending on the situation.

Pronunciation - Speak clearly, consider accents and level of language (using big words) inappropriate comments or gestures.

Enunciation - Over emphasise some words or statements for impact.

Repetition - Repeat key points or important areas.

Speed - Vary speed to influence delegates
- Faster delivery to excite, stimulate and energise
- Slow delivery to emphasise, dramatise and control

> You need your voice as a trainer, so learn to drink lots of water each day you deliver training. And always carry some throat pastilles with you just in case you need them.

USING SILENCE

Using silence is equally as powerful as using your voice. Are you confident to use silence? If you are not, then perhaps a little practice is required?

- When you ask delegates a question, learn not to jump straight in and rephrase if you don't get an immediate response. Use a timer and give them at least 15 seconds of silence before rephrasing.

- You might need to tell yourself that silence is not uncomfortable. Instead, silence is a positive thing as it gives people time to think. It also gives those delegates who like to reflect on questions, time to reflect and answer without someone else always jumping in first.

There is a useful brainstorming technique that many use that demonstrates the power of silence. If you have not come across this, here is how it works:

1. Imagine you are beginning a workshop on innovation and you start with an icebreaker designed to get delegates thinking creatively. Ask them to come up with as many uses of a piece or hunk of bread as they can (or paperclip, tyre, doughnut, matchstick etc).

2. Ask your delegates to shout out to the group their ideas and choose someone to flipchart them. Time them for one minute.

3. Then say that for one minute they must remain silent. No shouting out, instead they must think and reflect. They may if they wish write things down for themselves.

4. After the minute is up, give them another minute to shout out to the group all their ideas and for ideas to be flipcharted.

Some call this kind of exercise Start Stop. You have one minute of discussion followed by one minute of silence. As many times as you like until you call a halt to the exercise.

In most cases, you will be so impressed with the creative thinking that can occur when delegates have the time to think in silence, you will never again question the power of silence during training sessions!

BODY LANGUAGE

When training you need to consider your **P-E-O-P-L-E** !

Top tips

- Avoid using 'props' to play with (pens, glasses, paperclips)
- Don't have loose change in your pocket
- Don't wear clothes that are too tight or uncomfortable
- Be aware of your verbal 'tics'
- Avoid closed or tense body positions

Posture and gestures

Think about how you stand and sit. Back straight? No slouching?

Think about how you use hand gestures?

Would some see your hand gestures as too much or would some see them as too minimalistic?

Eye contact

Maintain good eye contact, but don't ever let it get to the point of staring.

Regularly sweep the group with your eyes but don't spend more than 2-3 seconds on any individual. 'Lighthouse effect'.

O — Orientation

Where is the best place for you to stand?

Will it help your presentation if you move around or will that distract delegates?

If you sit, will you lose impact or will you gain a sense of 'learning together'?

P — Proximity

How close do you stand to delegates?

Are any of them crowding you and do you need to move them back?

L — Looks/appearance

Make sure you have got your 'look' right for the event that you are running. Make sure you haven't gone too casual or too formal.

Check your 'look' on breaks to ensure you look professional rather than dishevelled.

E — Expressions of emotion

When do you use your facial expressions to express emotion?

It is far easier to listen to someone for a whole day who puts emotion into their voice than someone who doesn't.

USE OF FLIPCHARTS

Even with so much technology available, flipcharts continue to be an invaluable tool for most trainers. They can be wonderful aids for trainers but they can also be a delegate's worst nightmare! You need to make sure you use them right.

Before the training begins

- Place the flipchart where all delegates can see. Check for yourself whether delegates at the back can actually read it, there is nothing more frustrating than an exercise conducted via a flipchart that only two thirds of the room can see.

- Check you have enough pages for the training session you are delivering and that the last person to use it hasn't left scribbling across every page.

- Check that your flipchart pens actually work and are not about to dry up. Make sure all the colours you are using are visible from the back of the room.

- Prepare titles on the flip chart pages in advance of the training beginning. If it helps, also write small prompts in pencil on each page. You will be able to see and read these, but none of your delegates will.

When delivering the training

- Ensure each flipchart you create has a title – bordered or underlined
- Use bullet points when creating a list
- Use at least two colours but avoid writing in red (use it for underlining and emphasis only)
- Characters should be approximately 10cm high
- Avoid writing full sentences
- Have a (secret) supply of quality marker pens
- If you are artistic, use this skill! It will really liven up your flipcharts

- Never talk to the flipchart! After all, it is an inanimate object!
- If your handwriting is poor – get a delegate to write on the flipchart
- Put poor spelling down to 'flipchart dyslexia' – a genuine condition!

Flipchart horrors. A few of the things we have experienced first hand!

- You drag the flipchart to bring it closer to delegates during an exciting discussion, but your dragging causes the legs to fall off.
- You lean on the flipchart to make your point and then knock the whole thing over.
- You nominate a delegate to write on the flipchart only to discover you have nominated someone who can't spell. Never nominate anyone to write on the flipchart for you. Ask for volunteers.

USE OF EQUIPMENT

There are a whole heap of things that can go wrong with equipment, but hopefully the following gives you a little food for thought when preparing your training.

Projectors
- Use the projector before the training so you are familiar with the buttons, switches, bulbs, power supply etc.
- Delegates hate sitting there waiting while an incompetent trainer fiddles around trying to make something work
- Set up the projector before delegates arrive
- Turn the projector off when not in use. It's surprising how much background noise they make which can become wearing across a whole day. The background noise can be especially difficult if you have any delegates who struggle with their hearing
- Avoid turning the pc off that attaches to it, except at lunch
- Turn the projector on three minutes before you need it

Slides
- Vary the frames and colours used in slides. Delegates need the variety
- If you get your children to create your PowerPoint then bear in mind you might need to tone down the special effects, gizmos and gadgets before you use it. It can all get a bit much!
- Use large letters (not less than 24pt) remember that not everyone has perfect vision like you!
- Use at least one image/logo/graph on each visual – and please don't use generic clip art that everyone has seen a thousand times
- Keep it simple
- Know what a slide says before you show it and never read a slide to the delegates – would you like it being done to you?
- Use a 'reveal' technique on some slides – not all at once
- Avoid a repetitive style – use an element of surprise!

Computers

- Don't let someone set up a computer for you, then walk away without giving you the password. All too often computers go into energy saving mode leaving you unable to see or access your files until someone hunts down an IT person.
- As with projectors, set it up, play with it, check its power saving mode - all before delegates arrive.
- If you have been told a computer will be in the room for you – never believe it! Wherever possible take a laptop with you just in case.
- Don't assume that just because someone has supplied you with a computer that they will have supplied you with a power lead.

Tablets/iPads

- These are great for keeping your training notes and timings on, but be careful not to fiddle with them
- Turn the sound off before you begin
- To avoid any disruption, turn any communications you have uploaded off (i.e. Skype)
- Don't leave them lying around on the desk when you go for lunch
- Carry a charger with you

Smart boards

If you are going to use a smart board, make sure you are familiar with how to operate it.

- How to switch it on
- How to switch on the volume if you need this
- How to save information or switch to clean pages when you need them
- How to erase words and change colours
- How to link the smart board to your laptop

Internet connection

- Never assume the training room you are in will have Wi-Fi or an internet connection. You need to ask before the training.
- Never assume the internet connection you have been given access to, will work, or that it will work continuously throughout your session. Can you deliver your training without a connection if needs be?
- Check the connection before delegates arrive. It is really bad form to fiddle around with these things when delegates are watching you and if it's not going to work, you need to know and plan accordingly.
- Never assume the password you have been given to access the internet will work first time around. Check it before delegates arrive.
- If you want to view something on the internet, ensure you know how to enter full screen mode via the projector so your delegates are not squinting at something too small to be seen by the human eye.
- Be aware that many organisations do not allow you to upload from your memory stick onto their computers. You need check if the file needs to be emailed over prior to your training session, rather than count on accessing it via the web during the training.

PRESENTATION OF EXERCISES

There are so many skills required in training. The art of listening, the art of presenting, dealing with conflict, keeping order, facilitating discussions etc. It is no mean feat to deliver a successful training session – whatever others might say.

One of the essential skills of course is the ability to present and manage activities and exercises. If you have 20 minutes for your delegates to do an exercise that demonstrates the point you are making, the last thing you want is to spend 10 minutes explaining and re-explaining what it is you want them to do. Equally, you want them to get it right first time and with minimum fuss. This is where the skill comes in!

But if you mess this up, what can you expect?

Frustration: As trainers, we have all had to deal with delegates who sit in their groups whingeing about the exercise, instead of getting on with it because they remain unclear as to what is expected of them. It appears to be human nature to whinge rather than seek clarification, particularly if you have sent them away to break out rooms and seeking clarification would require someone standing up and coming to find you! Delegates' frustration then holds up your training and will mean that your delegates rapidly lose confidence in you.

Lost time: Another downside of not managing exercises well is you lose valuable time. Time is really precious and what you cannot do is overrun or get to the end of a task with key learning goals not having been achieved.

Energy: One of the great things about activities and exercises is that they often bring energy to the group. Allowing delegates to move around, to talk, to get involved raises energy levels so what you do not want to do is lose this opportunity to re-energise your delegates by messing up in your presentation of the exercise.

So here are a few tips on presenting exercises well...

- You might know what you want your delegates to do, but they do not, so you need to be really clear in your instructions.
- Ideally have written instructions to hand out, even if you plan to give verbal instructions first.
- Consider, when presenting the exercise, whether any delegates have a disability, language problem, learning difficulty, mobility issue that will affect their ability to do the exercise.
- Don't be put off by any delegates who tell you that your exercise puts them out of them comfort zone. Most of us only really learn when we are shoved far out of our comfort zones, so ask them to participate, but tell them you will support.
- If you change instructions for the exercise part way through (perhaps reduce or extend the timings for example) make sure that all delegates have heard you. Often people get so carried away in exercises, you could be shouting your instructions and they still wouldn't hear.
- Be careful of the words you use to avoid people misinterpreting your instructions. It will mess up the whole exercise. 'Fold the piece of paper' is a classic. There are probably 50 ways you could fold a piece of paper, so provide enough instruction to ensure that everyone ends up folding the paper in the same way.
- Allow delegates to ask questions of clarification, but be prepared to shut down any delegate who appears to be being deliberately obtuse and who is asking question after question. Some people behave like this in order to distance themselves from an exercise they do not want to participate in.

Half the challenge of delivering good training is developing the skills to work well with and manage a whole variety of delegates. Here is our quick overview of essential skills for trainers.

Score yourself against each of these skills below, on a scale of 1-10. 1 being poor and 10 being fantastic. So where are your strengths and weaknesses?

Your score

- Ability to think on your feet
- Ability to be assertive when necessary
- Ability to show empathy
- Ability to listen
- Great communication skills
- Ability to bring energy into a group
- Ability to concentrate for long periods
- Ability to innovate and create
- Ability to deal with conflict
- Good organisational skills

It would be highly unusual if you don't find all the groups you train are completely different: different dynamics; different strengths and different challenges. But life would be boring if you could predict who is going to walk through your door and how they are going to respond to your training, wouldn't it?

- Sometimes you might have a hostile group at the beginning, perhaps as a result of having been told to attend, rather than asked to attend.
- Sometimes you have a group who don't know each other and who seem to have no desire to gel.
- Sometimes you get one dominant, ego driven delegate who insists you are wasting their time and that they would rather be working. They then rudely use their mobile at every available opportunity and disrupt everyone else.
- Sometimes you get a group of delegates who are so diverse in their knowledge, experience or intelligence, that it is really hard to know how to even begin to deliver your material.

MANAGING YOUR DELEGATES

MANAGING YOUR DELEGATES

The list could go on, but it's not necessary. What is crucial is that you never get complacent about who is going to walk through your door and the fact that you need to have great skills to be able to welcome and manage them. Over the next few pages we take a look at the following:

- Understanding the different types of delegate
- Involving delegates
- Energising a group
- Dealing with conflict
- Questions and answers

UNDERSTANDING THE DIFFERENT TYPES OF DELEGATE

Ever come across any of these? Or is the more challenging question: ever been any of these?

DELEGATE TYPE	PROFILE	ACTION
THE HECKLER	<ul><li>Probably insecure</li><li>Perhaps bored generally with work</li><li>Gets satisfaction from irritating others</li><li>Aggressive and argumentative</li></ul>	<ul><li>Never get upset</li><li>Praise, express agreement, move on</li><li>Wait for a misstatement of fact and then throw it to the group for correction</li></ul>
THE TALKER/ KNOW IT ALL	<ul><li>A keen chatterbox</li><li>A show off</li><li>Well informed and eager to show it</li></ul>	<ul><li>At a pause, thank them, refocus and move on</li><li>Slow them down with a tough question</li><li>Jump in and ask the group for comment</li><li>Ask them if they can hold their questions until the end of the day so you can move on</li></ul>

MANAGING YOUR DELEGATES

MANAGING YOUR DELEGATES

DELEGATE TYPE	PROFILE	ACTION
THE GRIPER	• Feels 'hard done by' • Probably has a pet hate • Will use you as a scapegoat	• Get them to be specific • Explain you are there to be positive and constructive • Use peer pressure
THE WHISPERER 	• Doesn't understand – clarifying, translating • Sharing stories triggered by the training • Bored, mischievous or hypercritical	• Stop talking, wait for them to look up and 'non-verbally' ask for permission to continue • Ask if they have something relevant to share
THE LATE ONE 	• Arrives late and is late back from every break • Lacks respect • Doesn't appreciate the impact on the rest of the group	• Ask them politely to be back on time from the next break • Tell them how late they are and what the impact that has had on the group • Close the door and just start the session without them

MANAGING YOUR DELEGATES

DELEGATE TYPE	PROFILE	ACTION
THE FIDDLER OR THE TEXTER	• Either is bored or pretends to be bored • Stressed with work left behind • Rude • Seeking attention	• Ask them politely to switch off their phone or leave the room if its an important text • Ask them the next question which will require them to participate • Stop talking and wait for them to look up
THE SILENT ONE	• Timid, insecure, shy • Bored, indifferent • Silently protesting about having to attend • Feeling unable to keep up or understand, out of their depth	• Find out during the first break what is causing them to be silent • Gentle encouragement to participate
THE DEBATER	• Quick to criticise others views • Very direct with their comments • Plays devil's advocate to any reasonable idea • Argumentative	• Deal with them promptly • Take a non direct and non aggressive approach • Try to make them feel actively involved in the discussion

INVOLVING DELEGATES

It's often easy to create a rapport with the majority of your delegates. The challenge of course is to find a way to create rapport with **all** of them. You don't need to make them your best friends, but you do need them sufficiently on side that:

1. They don't derail the training for others
2. They don't distract or upset other delegates
3. They leave your course having learnt at least some of what you hoped they would learn

General rules for involving delegates:

- Treat delegates with physical or mental difficulties in the same way as others, but provide an opportunity for delegates to make you aware of any extra support required
- Avoiding using examples that may not be meaningful to everybody
- Change the group structures at each activity
- Consider encouraging different seating arrangements after a break/lunch
- Don't impose your own ethics or values in the training
- Never make sexist or racist jokes or comments
- Monitor delegates for anyone who may be having difficulty understanding
- Respect delegates personal space
- Be aware of situations that may embarrass individuals
- Be sensitive to hidden differences (e.g. sexuality, health conditions)
- When asking questions of the group, be conscious of giving opportunities to those who haven't contributed as much as others

And a few ideas for drawing in those who are not as involved as they need to be:

- Take them to one side during the first break and express your concern about their lack of involvement and ask for their ideas about what you can do to involve them
- Be clear with them about the effect their behaviour has on the rest of the group, give specific examples if possible
- Ask them if they understand why they are on the training course and talk through what might be in it for them
- Do not be bullied into allowing a delegate to remove their chair to the back of the room away from the group
- Be assertive with those who play with phones, take calls and overtly do other work in your training course
- If necessary, ask a delegate to leave the training as your priority is to create a positive learning environment for everyone

ENERGISING A GROUP

Years of experience have shown us that a group that is energised learns best. Delegates have longer periods of concentration, they are engaged with the learning, and they encourage and support each other.

In an ideal world your delegates will arrive ready and raring to go. More often than not though they will come in anxious, or unsure, or minds focussed back with the work on their desks, or yet to be convinced that time with you today will be a good use of their time.

Time for you to bring some energy in to the group! We will look at ways to do this in a few moments.

But first, there are several times during a training session when you need to be aware of low energy levels:

- When delegates first arrive
- Towards the lunch break when concentration is low, sugar levels down and hunger pangs starting to distract
- Immediately after lunch can also be a low point, particularly if delegates have been sat down throughout the lunch break
- Mid to late afternoon are other low points particularly if delegates are tired due to concentrating hard earlier in the day, were up early to travel to the training, or otherwise if they have been watching a PowerPoint presentation or similar

There are also several things that can cause energy to disappear:

- You talking too much
- You having a flat monotonous voice
- You being so focussed on being professional, that you forget to insert energy and enthusiasm
- Too much eye glazing PowerPoint
- Low lighting in the room

- Insufficient activity and movement
- A room that is too small and that starts to feel crowded after a few hours together
- Training materials that lack variety
- Having an energy vampire in the group (you know... they are the ones who endlessly moan and whinge and slowly everyone around them loses the will to live)

So what can you do to energise the group? Here are some of our ideas:

- Begin each new training session with a well thought through icebreaker
- If the delegates have been sitting down earlier on in the day, use an icebreaker that gets them on their feet
- If they don't know each other, use an icebreaker that gets them interacting
- In a break, privately challenge the energy vampire in the room to consider the impact their attitude has on others
- Use regular icebreakers and energisers
- Take an early break if that is not too disruptive
- Do something unexpected
- Change direction – do something different
- Open the window or take your training outside for a short period
- Deliver your training from the other end of the room, it will cause everyone to move around in their seats and possibly even get up and change seats
- Ask a delegate to take your place and run the next exercise
- Use your delegates during the day to do the flipchart writing for you
- Bring some refreshments into the room
- Make good use of break out space
- Banish the PowerPoint unless you can use one that lasts less than 10 minutes
- Take some voice coaching to minimise your impact on delegates in respect of energy levels

DEALING WITH CONFLICT

This might be your worst nightmare! Conflict comes in several guises:

- Those delegates who pick a fight with you (verbally!)
- Delegates who pick a fight with, or pick on, other delegates
- A delegate who has an emotional outburst
- Those delegates who refuse to take part in an activity
- Delegates who give you the silent treatment or who are deliberatively uncooperative or inattentive

> Each situation will present its own challenges but what you need to remember is that the other delegates will look to you to resolve the issue that is now affecting them all.

As a general rule, if someone interrupts or responds emotionally during a training session the best thing you can do is – **LISTEN**

They will soon calm down when they realise their behaviour is not being reciprocated, or you are not provoked by their behaviour, actions or words.

- If you want to explore their anger or emotion, ask questions to reflect back:

    - "You're upset with…"
    - "You're unhappy about…"
    - "So you are saying…"

- Show you are interested, but not defensive
- Allow them to confirm your interpretation of the outburst
- Quickly specify the problem and suggest a solution
- If you have inadvertently upset a delegate, apologise for offending them and move on – don't dwell on it.
- If a delegate leaves the training – let them go. Other delegates are involved and are waiting for your next step.

As a general rule, if someone is refusing to take part, or is giving you the silent treatment:

- Explore the reasons for this with them privately in the next break
- Gently encourage them to get involved
- Ask questions during discussions and activities to involve them
- Put them in groups with people who might support them and help them get involved
- Publicly, give them tasks to do

QUESTIONS – AND ANSWERS!

Questions

Being skilled at questioning is a great advantage as a trainer. You can use questions to continually engage your delegates, get them thinking, make them question what they are doing and why, creating an environment in which they can be appropriately challenged.

The key with questioning skills is to ask your question and then shut up! Never be tempted to fill the silence that your question creates, or to ease pressure on your delegates by providing the answer yourself. Ask your question, then its time for you to listen.

Encourage your delegates to ask questions too. The more questions they ask, the more engaged you will know they are and the more relevant you can make their learning.

HOW?   WHO?   WHERE?   WHAT?   WHEN?   WHY?

Avoid questions:

- Which are long and complicated
- That ask the same thing in three or four different ways
- That include assumptions on your part
- Which are vague
- Which allow the learner to guess
- That end with a question word

Reasons to ask group questions:

Every other statement that comes out of your mouth should be a question. Not all of them will require an answer. Questions can be used to:

- Energise
- Stimulate debate
- Introduce topics or change topic
- Share experiences
- Get delegates to reason
- To gauge understanding

Reasons to ask individual questions:

- Establish existing knowledge
- Recap on previous sessions
- Gain interest/improve engagement
- Maintain interest - keep them involved
- Check understanding and progress
- Encouragement - use why questions to reason things out rather than just give information

Questions throughout the training:

- Use: "Any questions?" at all stages of your learning session and encourage questions from delegates throughout.
- Waiting until the end of the session to invite questions may mean they will forget what they wanted to ask.

Dealing with difficult questions:

- Praise the questioner: "That's a really interesting/difficult question – well done"
- Reflect on the question: "If I understand correctly, you're asking…"
- Answer the question or deflect by using the group: "What do the rest of you think?" or "Has anyone had a similar problem?"
- Alternatively, deflect to a particular delegate: "Bill, you're an expert on this"

- Another option is to deflect back to the questioner: "You obviously have thought about this, what is your view?"
- If you or any of the delegates are unable to answer the question satisfactorily, say you will find out and get back to them. Find out as soon as possible and share your findings to the whole group.

Answers

Dealing with answers

ANSWER	ACTION	WORDS

CORRECT ANSWER — Praise appropriate to the individual — "That's right" / "Well done" / "Well remembered" / "Good answer"

WRONG ANSWER — Ensure they know it is not the right answer, get them to reason out why it is wrong rather than give the right answer immediately — "That's not the answer I'm looking for, why did you say that?"

ANSWER	ACTION	WORDS
 PARTIALLY CORRECT	Confirm the part that is correct, help the learner reason out the part that is incorrect	"You're partly right… but think about…"
 NO ANSWER	Rephrase the question, give examples, encourage, prompt	"Perhaps I didn't phrase that very well…" "Do you remember when…?"

MANAGING YOUR DELEGATES

WAYS TO SPLIT A GROUP

It is amazing how much the dynamics in the room can change if people sit in certain places. On every training course, part of the learning comes from the sharing of knowledge and ideas between delegates. As the trainer, you need to ensure that the group dynamics are right and that the delegates are arranged in groups that maximise learning and participation.

When first arriving for a course, delegates will often choose to sit next to those they know already or those they feel they will have an affinity with. At times you will permit this, but at other times you may choose to actively move delegates to change the dynamic in the room.

If you want to regularly change where delegates sit:

- Give each delegate a number around the room – then for example, say those with an even number will work together and those with odd numbers will form team two etc.
- Split by work discipline or departments
- Split by choice – they decide the groups
- Force a move by saying they can sit where they like but not where they were before the break
- Change the desk layout over lunch so when they return different groups will have to form, 'cruel to be kind' is how we view this approach!

In managing a learning environment you need to consider the following:

(Before you even book the training room you intend to use)

- Lighting
- Room temperature/air con
- Availability of water
- Distracting features around the room
- Space for delegates to work or spread their papers
- Comfort of seats
- Room for restless delegates to stand up and stretch
- Break out room availability
- Power sockets for charging phones
- Security of your delegates possessions if they are left in the room during lunch breaks

You should also consider mobile phone reception – there can be nothing more stressful for some delegates than having no Wi-Fi or phone reception. Equally you might deliberately choose a venue with no phone reception or Wi-Fi, but be prepared to deal with some disgruntled delegates!

OTHER THINGS TO CONSIDER

- Will the room you are in give you the space you need for your activities and exercises?
- Will any of your activities be noisy and if so, what impact will this have on those in rooms nearby?
- Is there outside space you can use on a sunny day?
- Will bringing refreshments and lunch in the room disrupt the entire course? Do you need to leave instructions for them to be brought in at certain times?

RUNNING ACTIVITIES AND EXERCISES

A few tips

- Make your brief clear to avoid delegates being confused, not understanding or feeling embarrassed they do not know what you expect of them
- Create an open, but 'safe' atmosphere
- Give positive reinforcement and verbally 'receive' all contributions
- Pick up non verbal messages from delegates and act upon them so delegates know you are observing and supporting even when they have said nothing
- Leave the groups to work alone and avoid interrupting unless they are going completely off course
- When it suits for certain tasks, act as time monitor for groups, but don't get actively involved
- Don't leave groups alone for too long during a task, it will leave them with the impression you have gone for a coffee break
- Facilitate feedback and ask each group to feed back on outcomes (either verbally or using the flipchart)
- Listen to everything that is said and ask for clarification if needed
- Ask other delegates if they would like to add anything
- Consolidate learning by summarising what outcomes you have achieved from each activity, link back to where you are in the course contents
- If using cameras or video recording, ensure delegates are aware of this and are comfortable with it, and if necessary reassure delegates of what will happen to photos and video recordings after the end of the training

SCENARIOS OR ROLE PLAYS

Firstly, avoid scenario or role play activities too early in a course. The group need to feel comfortable working together and they will feel more inclined to 'act' out scenarios if they don't feel any pressure. You will always find some delegates who are more extroverted and may actively enjoy this type of activity, involve them initially and as other more introverted delegates understand the process, they may feel like getting involved – although they shouldn't feel too pressured!

Prepare in advance
- The required number of handouts
- Use coloured paper or highlighters to show different scenarios
- Think about delegates beforehand and allocate groups working with their strengths

Make sure your brief is clear and in writing
- Where delegates can be creative or ad lib, explain what this means
- Ensure everyone knows what is expected
- Seek verbal feedback and reassurance

Feed back to delegates
- Ask the participants, in turn, how they feel
- Recap on what happened (preferably use notes)
- Give constructive feedback
- Use the other delegates to feed back

In giving feedback
- Use a praise 'sandwich' to praise what went well, to give feedback on areas of improvement (avoid more than two) and to praise and thank them for taking part
- Never give feedback you couldn't take yourself
- Base all your feedback on factual evidence
    - "When you said..."
    - "What do you think the member of staff felt when you..."
    - "Why did you do/say that"

Delegate rules of scenario/practical exercises
- You are allowed to make mistakes
- You are allowed to be embarrassed
- It is not a real work situation – be creative
- Be as realistic as you can, respond as the character you have been given
- When being the manager – be yourself
- Feedback is encouraged from everyone but must be constructive
- Enjoy it and laugh if you need to

ICEBREAKERS AND ENERGISERS

INTRODUCTION

Before running a training session, you might like to begin with a short exercise to grab the attention of your delegates and get them working together. There are many icebreaker and energiser exercises on the market to buy and you will also find many available free on the internet. But make sure you choose good ones that are tried and tested, as you don't want to lose the attention of your delegates before you have even begun! To get you started, we have put together a small selection of some of our favourites, including some created by the Jaluch team.

But first just a few words about icebreakers and energisers:

ICEBREAKERS

It is sensible, advisable and also generally beneficial to start each new training course with an icebreaker. Even when delegates have all worked closely together in the normal work environment, working together in a training environment is actually a very different experience, so taking some time to get people feeling comfortable is really valuable.

Icebreakers can be used for many purposes such as:
- Relaxing anxious delegates
- Introducing delegates to your training style and setting the tone
- Introducing the training topics
- People who don't know each other can begin to learn about each other and understand how to work together
- Providing an opportunity for delegates who know each other a little, to learn more about each other
- Creating a 'transition' for delegates to switch out of normal work mode and into training mode.

INTRODUCTION

ENERGISERS

Research shows that delegates can begin to lose their concentration after just 20 minutes!

If you're taking the time to present material to delegates then clearly it's crucial you ensure your delegates are awake and focussed enough throughout your training, to take on board what you are saying and fully participate in exercises. This is where energisers become invaluable.

Energisers can be particularly helpful if they get delegates onto their feet and moving around. If energisers include a little fresh air, then the benefits can be even greater! Experience has shown us that even just a five minute energiser can dramatically improve the concentration and engagement levels of delegates.

If you are interested in buying further icebreakers and energisers from Jaluch, we sell an icebreaker and energiser book, available from: **www.jaluch.co.uk/trainingstore**

ICEBREAKERS AND ENERGISERS

TOWER OF TROUBLE

Time required: 20 min

Overview: A fun exercise to get delegates working together. In this exercise delegates are asked to work in groups to build a tower made out of paper. The tallest tower wins the prize! The element of competition in this exercise often brings out lots of energy. Changing the goal posts in respect of the materials they have to work with after they have done the planning stage, provides an opportunity to see how they react and respond to change.

Learning objective/s: Working as a team; working to strengths; problem solving; creative thinking; team communication; planning and preparation; dealing with change.

What you will need:
- Plain A4 paper
- Sticky tape, cut into one inch strips
- Some blu or white tack rolled into marble sized pieces
- Small prize for the winning team (if you want one)
- Pens (any sort, any style)
- Timer
- Handout 1

TRAINER NOTE

You could use this as an icebreaker at the start of session, otherwise as an energiser, or introduction to the topic of team working or problem solving.

You will need to split your delegates into several smaller groups. We would recommend each group has a minimum of three and a maximum of four.

As this exercise involves building, we suggest you make sure there is enough clear table space and enough room for delegates to stand and work. If there is enough space for groups to work in different parts of the room, it's a bonus, because it minimises opportunities for groups to complain that other groups are stealing their ideas!

There is lots of learning opportunity in this exercise, so you are able to decide where you want the focus to be, for example: on problem solving and creativity; or on team working and team communication.

Before you explain what they must do, handout to each group: 10 sheets of A4 paper, five strips of sellotape, three pieces of blu-tack and one pen.

You will then explain what they need to do, but at the end of the planning phase and before the building phase begins, we suggest you throw a spanner in the works by going round the tables and removing, at random, selected materials from each group (e.g. group one loses three bits of sellotape, two pieces of A4 and a ball of blu-tack, group two loses four pieces of A4 and one piece of sellotape, group three loses all its blu-tack and so on).

Get ready for cries of derision and 'not fair' - you will be the most despised person in the room at this point!

There are three stages in this exercise - 10 minutes for planning, five minutes for building and then one minute to check that the tower stays up!

If you want to, you may decide to award a small prize to the winning team (based on height of tower).

DELEGATE INSTRUCTIONS

Your task is to build the tallest free standing tower, using only the materials you have been given.

At the end of the exercise, your tower must stand for at least one minute, unsupported.

At the start there will be 10 minutes planning for each group during which time you cannot begin to build.

When you give the go ahead at the end of the 10 minutes delegates will have five minutes to build, at the end of which time the tower will need to stand up on its own for a full one minute.

TRAINER DEBRIEF INSTRUCTIONS

For a short exercise there are many things that you can choose to focus on here however some of our ideas for a debrief are:

- How disruptive was it to have some of your resources taken away - impact on plans/performance/morale/stress? Also, what sort of behaviours were seen as a result?
- How might you have used the 10 mins 'planning' differently if you knew that some of your resources would be taken away?
- How many finished planning early, confident they had it 'nailed' with their design, only to have this confidence stripped away from them?
- Did all groups feel that everyone in each group was equally valued in planning and creating this tower?
- Did each team choose a leader or did some go for group consensus? Which was more successful?
- In hindsight, did each group feel that they had been creative enough in their approach?
- What are delegates thoughts on how they individually responded to the change in plan, when resources were removed?

TOWER OF TROUBLE HANDOUT (1)

Each groups aim is to build the tallest free standing tower, using the materials provided.

Only these materials can be used to build your tower. **These are the resources you have been given:**

- Plain A4 paper
- Sticky tape, cut into one inch strips
- Some blu or white tack rolled into marble sized pieces

At the start there will be 10 minutes planning for each group, during this time you cannot begin to build. You then will have five minutes to build, at the end of which time the tower will need to stand up on its own for a full one minute, unsupported.

YOUR NOTES

UNCONCIOUS BIAS – IT'S NOT A GAME

Time required: 20 min

Overview: An exercise designed to challenge thinking around bias and inclusion. Presented in a light-hearted format, the content of this exercise probes some really important areas around thinking, behaviours and bias. In this exercise delegates working in groups are asked to spend time discussing an infographic on unconscious bias. They are also asked to assess the impact of bias in their own organisations.

Learning objective/s: Thinking about bias and inclusion; assessing the impact of bias on the organisation.

What you will need:
- Access to the internet to project the infographic onto a screen **OR** Delegates to access the infographic via their own mobile devices
- Handout 2

Infographic: http://www.jaluch.co.uk/infographic/

TRAINER NOTE

This exercise can be used either during, or at the start of a session on inclusion or diversity. It might also be an interesting icebreaker at the start of a session around team building or team working given the number of questions and thoughts it might raise.

We suggest you organise delegates into groups of two or three. To have a good discussion, four in a group is probably the largest size you could work with.

You will be asking delegates to look at an infographic that Jaluch has created on unconscious bias. This can be accessed using the link, via the **Jaluch.co.uk** website, or by scanning this QR code:

You will ask delegates to look at and discuss the infographic. Questions to prompt their discussion are included in the handout.

We would suggest you give delegates 15 minutes to read and discuss and then five minutes for a quick debrief. There is the potential to expand this into a much longer exercise, if that suits your purposes.

DELEGATE INSTRUCTIONS

Please take a look at the infographic on unconscious bias that I will give you a link to/is on the screen.

In your groups, I would like you to read through the infographic and discuss the questions set out in the handout.

You have 15 minutes to talk this through so try not to get into any really meaty discussions, but take more of an overview of the information that has been presented.

We will then have about five minutes to hear some of your thoughts when we reform the full group.

TRAINER DEBRIEF INSTRUCTIONS

- What were your initial thoughts and impressions on the infographic information?
- Is there one area from the subjects covered that you think is particularly relevant to this organisation?
- Did anything particularly surprise you?
- What ideas do you have for what we might do to minimise the effects of unconscious bias in this organisation?
- I would like each of you to identify one thing that you could do more/less of in the coming days/weeks to work in a more inclusive way
- Do you believe that this organisation has an inclusive approach to managing staff or are there certain groups who tend to be excluded?

UNCONCIOUS BIAS HANDOUT (2)

Take 15 minutes to look through the infographic that can be accessed at the following address: **www.jaluch.co.uk/infographic** or by scanning this QR code:

Here is a guide to what you might discuss in your group:
- What were your initial thoughts and impressions on the infographic information?
- Is there one area from the subjects covered that you think is particularly relevant to this organisation?
- Did anything particularly surprise you?
- What ideas do you have for what we might do to minimise the effects of unconscious bias in this organisation?
- If each of you could identify one thing that you could do more/less of in the coming days/weeks to work in a more inclusive way, what would it be?
- Do you believe that this organisation has an inclusive approach to managing staff or are there certain groups who tend to be excluded?

YOUR IDEAS AND THOUGHTS

DOWN THE MOUNTAIN

Time required: 10-15 min

Overview: This exercise encourages delegates to go back to basics and think about the technology they have. A recluse has just descended from his cave at the top of a mountain where he has been meditating for the past 10 years. Your delegates meet him at the bottom of the mountain and he immediately asks what this contraption is that they are holding. So they now need to explain to him what an iPhone is, what it does and why it is important to them. They will work in two groups for this exercise, with one person in each group electing to act the part of the 'recluse'.

Learning objective/s: Going back to basics with technology; learning how to be clear and concise in explanations; communicating as a group; practising training or teaching techniques.

What you will need:
- Delegates' personal iPhones – at least one per group
- Handout 3

TRAINER NOTE

You might need to forewarn delegates that there will be an exercise using smartphones, just in case someone does not bring one to the training room.

This exercise is ideally done with delegates working in two groups, although if you have a larger group you might split them into three.

You will be asking delegates to take five minutes to explain to their 'recluse' what an iPhone is, what it does and why it is important to them.

You might find that: delegates talk over each other; they repeat what others have said; seek to provide explanations to what others have said; some may say nothing or use so much modern jargon in their explanation that no recluse would understand at all.

All of this is information that you can use in your debrief.

If you wanted to use the exercise a second time to demonstrate some of the points you cover in your initial debrief, consider putting them into much smaller groups (just two with each 'recluse') and setting them the challenge of being much clearer in their explanations second time around.

DELEGATE INSTRUCTIONS

In this short exercise, I would like you to split into two groups.

A recluse has just descended from his cave at the top of a mountain, where he has been meditating for the past 10 years.

You meet at the bottom of the mountain and he immediately asks what this contraption is that you are holding. So now you need to explain to him what an iPhone is, what it does and why it is important to you.

You will work in two/three groups for this exercise with one person in each group electing to act the part of the 'recluse'.

Your challenge is to keep it simple, bear in mind what technology looked like when your 'recluse' was last in the real world, working as a team to educate and enlighten him.

The 'recluse' in your group should feel free to enjoy testing your ability to provide clear explanations!

TRAINER DEBRIEF INSTRUCTIONS

You could debrief delegates using some of the following ideas:

- How did the 'recluses' feel about the quality of explanations given to them?

- How did the others feel about the quality of their explanations?

- What jargon was used that people don't even recognise as jargon any more?

- What explanations were given about what the 'I' stands for in iPhone, iPad etc?

- How convincing were the reasons given why people chose to have an iPhone?

- Did one person monopolise the discussion?

- What prevented concise and clear explanations being given?

DOWN THE MOUNTAIN HANDOUT (3)

A recluse has just descended from his cave at the top of a mountain where he has been meditating for the past 10 years.

You meet him at the bottom of the mountain and he immediately asks what this contraption is that you are holding. So now you need to explain to him:

- What an iPhone is
- What it does
- Why it is important to you

One person in your group needs to volunteer to act the part of the 'recluse'.

Your challenge is to keep it simple, bear in mind what technology looked like when your 'recluse' was last in the real world and work as a team to educate and enlighten him.

The 'recluse' in your group should feel free to enjoy testing your ability to provide clear explanations!

NOTES FOR YOUR EXPLANATION

What is an iPhone?

What does it do?

Why do you choose to have one?

WALLPAPER

Time required: 10 min

Overview: A quick and easy energiser, this exercise asks delegates to take a photo of something within the training room (it could be themselves) and make this the wallpaper on their iPads, phones or tablets.

Learning objective/s: Gaining confidence with technology; creativity; working with other delegates.

What you will need:
- Delegates' iPhones, smartphones, iPads or tablets (one is needed for each delegate)
- Prize for the winning wallpaper if you want to award a prize!
- Handout 4

TRAINER NOTE

You might need to forewarn delegates that there will be an exercise using iPhones and iPads just in case someone does not bring one to the training room. It might be useful to have some spare chargers with you.

This exercise is ideally done with delegates working on their own although it can be done with delegates working in pairs. This might be sensible if delegates are particularly lacking in confidence with technology.

You will be asking delegates to take just five minutes to:

1) Use the camera on their phone to take a photo of something interesting in the training room and then

2) Load it up as their wallpaper.

ICEBREAKERS AND ENERGISERS

DELEGATE INSTRUCTIONS

In this short exercise, I would like you to each take a photo of something of interest in the room. Be creative! You need to use your smartphones or tablets for this. You will then need to load up your photo as your new wallpaper.

In this exercise we are interested developing your confidence with using technology and using it to be creative. You have five minutes to take your photo and load it up as your wallpaper.

TRAINER DEBRIEF SUGGESTIONS

You could debrief delegates using some of the following ideas:

- How did delegates feel about this exercise? Did they enjoy it?
- Who came up with the best picture? What did they do that others did not?
- How familiar are delegates with using their 'settings' options?
- Are there any settings that delegates have never explored? If not, why not?
- Is there any training that the organisation could provide to staff to ensure greater familiarity with the technology that is used during the working day?

WALLPAPER HANDOUT (4)

1. Take a photo

You have just five minutes to take a photo using the camera app on your mobile device. Be creative, but you must find something within the training room to photograph.

2. Load your wallpaper

Once you have taken your photo, load it up as your new wallpaper. If you are not familiar with doing this, you can find your wallpaper option in 'settings'.

3. Things to ponder while you do this exercise

> What other options in 'settings' are you not familiar with?
>
> How many of your colleagues feel comfortable and confident when using their mobile devices?
>
> Do you feel comfortable being asked to be creative in taking a photo for your wallpaper? If not, what makes you feel uncomfortable about being asked to be creative?

© Copyright Jaluch Limited 2013

CANDIDATE SEARCH

Time required: 15 min

Overview: This exercise provides an opportunity for delegates to use the audio recorder function on their phone or iPad. The challenge is to record a 60 second summary of why people should come to work in your organisation. It's a chance to practise communication and presentation skills, as well as to think about how you present your organisation to the outside world.

Learning objective/s: Gaining familiarity with technology; creating clear communication messages; presentation skills.

What you will need:

- Delegates' iPhones or iPads
- 60 second timer for presentations
- Handout 5

TRAINER NOTE

You might need to forewarn delegates that there will be an exercise using mobile devices just in case someone does not bring one to the training room. It might be useful to have some spare chargers with you.

So often, employees use only a fraction of the available functionality on their phones. This exercise provides an opportunity to use the audio recording function.

This is a good energiser because delegates should have fun doing this. It can also be used as an icebreaker if you use the exercise primarily for delegates to begin to work together.

A perfect exercise if you are running recruitment and selection training. Good also for use during training on communication skills.

Not sure how to put your delegates into groups? To avoid delegates always working with those they know best, why not go around the room and allocate numbers 1,2,3 and 4 to everyone. You can then ask all those who were given '1' to work together, all '2's to work together etc.

DELEGATE INSTRUCTIONS

In groups of two or three, I would like you to take one iPhone or iPad and make a 60 second audio recording. Your recording should aim to 'sell' this organisation to any prospective recruitment candidates.

You have five minutes to make your recording so you need to be organised and work efficiently as a team.

The audio recording function should be available as a pre loaded app. If you can't find it, look under 'utilities'.

Think about what message you want to give and how to clearly get that message across.

Further detail is given on Handout 5.

TRAINER DEBRIEF INSTRUCTIONS

In this exercise, there are lots of debrief options, but here are a few of our ideas:

Whose was the best recording? What made it the best?

How many key messages can you get across in 60 seconds?

Does the organisation communicate well to prospective candidates?

Does the information on the website and the way managers behave provide a consistent message to candidates?

What are the key things that you ought to avoid when trying to communicate via an audio message?

CANDIDATE SEARCH HANDOUT (5)

In today's environment it can be very hard to recruit great people.

Often adverts attract so many candidates it is hard to sift through to find the good ones. Sometimes adverts just attract the wrong type of candidate, leaving you with no choice at all.

This is your chance to make a 60 second recording that will be posted on the jobs section of your organisation's website for prospective candidates to listen to.

You need to 'sell' your organisation.

Areas to think about:
Introduction
Key message/s
Language used
Sound effects used
Conclusion and call to action

AUDIO RECORDING PLAN

AND FINALLY...

Training is challenging and demanding, but extremely rewarding, so enjoy the role! At Jaluch, we always say that it is on those occasions when a delegate writes to us after a course and says that we inspired them, we know we have done a great job. Then we can go home with a great big smile on our face. How fantastic is that!

> A golden rule is to always seek to deliver a course that you yourself would be energised to attend.

As with everything though, becoming a skilled trainer is a matter of continuous improvement, so seek feedback on your training style and skills from delegates and use their feedback to work out where to focus your energies in developing your style and skills.

Just one note of warning: If you find yourself denying the relevance/importance of feedback from a delegate, just take a step back and really challenge yourself about whether your reaction to the feedback is a reaction you would permit from one of your delegates!

Feeling as though there is a lot to learn? Well there is if you want to be a great trainer! As long as you are continuously learning that is all that counts. Perhaps this quote will spur you on in your learning?

> "The road to success is lined with many tempting parking spaces."
> Anonymous

AND FINALLY...

On a cautionary note though, don't ever aim just to emulate someone else - some other trainer you know and admire. Be proud of who you are and all of us at Jaluch would encourage you to seek to develop your own style as a trainer. There is room in the training profession for all styles and all personalities. Welcome on board!

How did we do?

Do you like this Trainers' Book but would like us to add in more topics? We'd love to hear your ideas so please email us: help@jaluch.co.uk

About Jaluch

Jaluch is a British HR and Training Consultancy with loads of personality and a sense of fun. We are opinionated, love to have a laugh and we thrive on straight talking. As a team we are always seeking to develop our skills and do our job even better tomorrow.

You can never learn enough and every day brings new experiences.

Jaluch supports hundreds of companies of all shapes and sizes both in the UK and further afield. We support organisations with both day to day HR advice and also learning and development programmes.

MORE FROM JALUCH

At Jaluch we offer a wide range of resources to support learning and development activities. These include:

Training Blasts

A monthly 2 minute update by email on a topic related to learning and development. Practical, pragmatic and designed to prompt fresh thinking.

If you'd like to sign up visit: **www.jaluch.co.uk/training-blast**

Training courses and one-to-one coaching sessions including:

- Managing with confidence
- Self presentation skills
- Developing supervisory skills
- Developing leadership skills
- Understanding our own preferred communication and behavioural styles
- Customer Service skills
- Giving constructive feedback
- Diversity and inclusion
- Unconscious bias
- Managing and motivating teams

Online assessment tools:

- Psychometric testing
- 360 degree leadership feedback
- General intelligence assessment
- Emotional intelligence assessment

eBooks

Managing Staff Absence - edited by Helen Jamieson
Managing Staff Performance - edited by Helen Jamieson

Currently available from: **www.amazon.co.uk**

AND FINALLY...

Training Kits

We have packaged up a number of our training courses so that trainers can just pick up our material and then deliver courses themselves in-house. Easy, practical, no time consuming preparation of materials and handouts, all provided on a USB stick just ready to be printed out and then handed out!

Our Bags of Learning have been designed for both professional trainers and also those in HR or Management who have been tasked with delivering a certain course. You do not have to be a professional trainer to use these materials. Included in our great Bags of learning are comprehensive trainers notes, pens, flipchart markers, games and exercises, a USB stick with all the handouts and some of them even have timers, bells and hooters if those are needed for the exercises. We've had great feedback on them.

Six hours of material in each bag that can be delivered in one day or across six separate sessions.

- Managing Absence
- Managing Performance
- Managing Discipline and Dismissals
- Managing Grievances
- Diversity and Inclusion
- 50 Icebreakers and Energisers for iPad and iPhone

Bags of Learning are currently available from:
www.jaluch.co.uk